Radically Condensed Instructions for Being Just as You Are

J Jennifer Matthews

1

Contents

Acknowledgments

For your dedicated support, I would like to thank the faculty of the Episcopal Divinity School and the philosophy faculties of the University of Louvain and Bard College.

For your constant support and loving encouragement, heartfelt thanks to my parents, Don and Katrina, my sister, Anne, and my partner, Mark.

This book is dedicated to my daughter, Alexandra.

Preface

I believe everyone deserves to have the book they are considering reading summed-up in five sentences. For all I know, five sentences are all you have time for. You may, for example, presently be in an office chair that is rolling off a cliff.

Even if you are not in such unfortunate circumstances, you should never be required to read more than five sentences. You don't know me and I have done nothing to earn your patience.

In five sentences, then:

This book is grounded in philosophical thinking known as 'Non-Dualism' or 'Non-Duality.'

It may be helpful to you.

However, you don't really need it.

You have already read dozens of books which are capable of reorienting you toward the mystery and poignancy of present-moment experience.

It is easy to see this mystery,
but tricky to stay with it.

Staying with it requires careful
examination of the assumptions that
pull us away.

Alright, alright.
One of the sentences ran on a bit.

Hey, where are you going?

Introduction

There is clarity: luminous, still and silent clarity. It is with you and in you. It *is* you. It always exists. No it never takes a break; no it never goes out for just one cigarette. It is the wholeness you can never fall out of. Not in your drunkest, sorriest, most hysterical moments, not even then can you fall out of this clear and sacred perfection. You know that.

You also know there is an ultimate and powerful truth which calls us to itself. It is everywhere. And no "where" - nowhere you can point to and say, "there it is!" At the same time, there is nothing else. Oh, except you.

And then there's you. In your heart of hearts you just don't get it, do you? You say, "I get it, I get it. I know I need to dissolve this heavy ego, this heavy problem. I know I have to let go. Of my concepts and my stuckness. I know I just need to "be here now." Oh and let go of this heavy self-centered trip of my self-enclosed existence. And all my other trips. And I know, I know. I know there's no way to "do" it, this letting go. Because that would be another project for my heavy, self-enclosed, self-deluded self. But just tell me, just quickly, what do I do?"

Radically Condensed Instructions
for Being Just As You Are

It's not your fault. Attempts to explain the clarity, stillness, and openness at the heart of existence often amount to what the philosophers call *'Ignotum per Ignotius:'* an explanation that is even more obscure than the thing it is trying to explain. This clarity, this openness, is not an easy subject to write or read about. Some folks have written eloquently, nonetheless, about the prime importance of recognizing this clarity in the here-and-now. (Ram Dass, Thich Nhat Hanh, and Eckhart Tolle, to give just three examples.)

Others have pointed out intelligently that we never really leave the clarity of the here-and-now. That our apparent exits into worry and regret only *seem* to take us out of the present moment. We can never remove ourselves from the present moment, however, no matter what we do. This is because the present moment, or (we could say) the present encounter, is the only encounter there is. (Peter Dziuban, Greg Goode, and Ken Wilber, to give just three examples.)

I would like to demystify the difference between these points, and remove some of our sense of conundrum, with the following idea: our return to the mystery and intimacy of the present moment doesn't have to be thought of as a goal, and certainly not a distant one. It is more like a lifestyle choice. We don't, I hope, celebrate Valentine's Day in the belief that we will eventually "get it." And we certainly don't celebrate Valentine's Day in the hope that we will never have to celebrate Valentine's Day again!

When it comes to returning to the present moment, however, our techniques often have this built-in redundancy. We return to the mystery and intimacy of the present moment, often in the hope that we will "awaken." I am offering the idea that when we are alive to the mystery and intimacy of the present moment, we are already awake. I am also in support of the latter argument, the "we can never leave the present moment" argument.

Being awake to the mystery of the present moment does not have a different ontological status than being asleep to it. This is just a way of saying that by being awake to the present moment, we are not adding anything to our existence. There *is* a felt difference, though, isn't there? Doesn't "being awake" feel different from "being asleep?" Where does this felt difference come from, and what does it mean?

Radically Condensed Instructions

When it comes to our spiritual lives, we are not just going for a change in feeling. We are going for a profound shift in our attitude and understanding. And yet this profound shift in understanding can actively prevent us from bothering ourselves, distracting ourselves, and in all other ways removing ourselves from felt contact with present-moment experience.

Let me give two Boston Zen koans as examples. (A Boston Zen koan, by the way, is just a koan that I, a Bostonian, made up.)

A Zen student says to her teacher:
"I am unclear about the nature of reality." Her teacher, an elderly Japanese gentleman, falls over his chair.

> Student: "Are you OK ?"
> Teacher: "Of course!"
> Student: "What on earth happened?"
> Teacher: "I resolved your lack of clarity about the nature of reality."

> The next day, as they are eating dinner:
> Student: "Please pass the salt."
> Teacher: "I see you are clear now about the nature of reality!"

In the first koan, the teacher tries to show that his student is troubling herself with thoughts about the nature of reality. When he falls over his chair, she is galvanized in the here-and-now by her concern for him and her desire to help. Her concerns about the 'nature of reality' are abstract and unnecessary by contrast. So abstract, in fact, that her teacher can resolve the whole pickle just by bringing her attention back to the present moment.

In the second koan, the student behaves in a sane and functional manner. In doing so, she demonstrates she has a perfectly fine understanding of the nature of reality. At least when she is not bothering herself with abstract concepts about the nature of the reality! How do these examples clarify the relationship between the constant and inalterable presence of Awareness, and our feeling of being awake?

When we are not in meditation, contemplation, or Satsang – when "ordinary life" resumes with its problems – we are tempted to think we have lost contact with Awareness. We think the sequence of events goes like this: we lose a serene and mystical feeling, then we are disturbed by our loss. The actual sequence of events, however, is that we *start* to bother ourselves, *then* we appear to lose the state of open awareness which is our very nature and the only experience there is. We "lose" it because we no longer allow it to register.

A feeling of peaceful and poignant openness associates with an accurate and clear understanding of the nature of things. The fact that we feel disturbed or bothered is actually the litmus test for this feeling, because it demonstrates the presence of a pre-existing, peaceful poignancy. If we did not have this peaceful and open state as our default, compared to what would we feel troubled or distressed?

Our essential openness is like a buoy which appears to sink under the surface of our conscious experience only when we are actively pushing it down. Please do not take even this image too literally. The fact is, our openness never really goes away, not even apparently. This concept is a little hard to grasp, isn't it? I don't know about you, but this is where my understanding sort-of collapses. This is it - the cosmic "*huh*?"

Let's take a look at what is going on here. Why do we feel distracted from our primary and continual existence as Awareness? What exactly is going on? Life is the most incredible mystery. Yet there is a collusion out there that life is something ordinary, and that we understand it. At least some of it. Well, at the very least, we think there is a clear "us" to understand it, and a clear "it" to be understood.

The Conspiracy of the Ordinary

The collusion that life is something ordinary, what I like to call "the conspiracy of the ordinary," causes us an enormous amount of unnecessary distraction. What is this conspiracy, and what can we do about it? I am going to introduce the following ideas. I've numbered them so you know I mean business:

1) We feel numb and separate from our lives as if we are living behind a pane of glass. We feel restless and blah. We can call this feeling "dissatisfaction."

2) We fail to appreciate the mystery of life. Because of this, we find ourselves wanting things to be different. We pursue external and internal goals in an effort to make things different. But this does not work. Our failure to appreciate the mystery inherent in our current situations, and our consequent attempts to transcend or improve them, causes our dissatisfaction.

3) There is good news. We *can* stop trying to get something *out* of life. It *is* possible to stop our obsession with transcending and improving our current situations.

4) We *can* be awake and intimately in touch with the mystery of the present moment. This is a lifestyle choice, not a goal. When something appears to take us out of present-moment experience, we can question it rather than follow it with credulity. We don't have to let it hoodwink us with the promise that we will be in touch with the mystery of present-moment experience when we've received what we want in the future, in another city or at another job.

5) We *can* understand philosophically that present-moment experience is all there is. This understanding is supremely important. We need to have a theoretical grasp of how it can be that what is right here and right now is really all there is. Otherwise we will be easily hoodwinked and will pin our hopes on distant external goals such as jobs, partners, and accomplishments, or on distant internal goals such as enlightenment. This understanding should also be viewed as a kind of ladder. We do not have to study philosophical ideas endlessly and become absorbed in their intricacies. As soon as we have used this ladder to reach the mystery of the present moment, we can kick it away.

Let's take a look at these ideas.

Idea 1 – We feel numb and separate from our lives as if we are living behind a pane of glass.

Some have called these feelings of dissatisfaction the "reactive emotions." I will define "reactive emotions" as natural reactions to a distorted and untrue picture of life. We think we are independent, self-subsisting entities who look out on an external world, from which we are separated by a metaphysical gap, which I have compared to a pane of glass. We think we also look in on, and act upon, an internal world. This picture of things is artificial and artificially limiting. We will discuss it further later on. For now it's enough to say that the reactive emotions are artificial limits, circumscribing an artificial bubble of self.

When we talk about the reactive emotions, we are recognizing the subtle difference between attempting to abandon present-moment experience, and living in appreciation of the mystery at the heart of experience. The self, or the activity of 'selving,' is characterized by a search for something we think is missing.

'Selving' is a misunderstanding which causes us to problematize our experience. As soon as we postulate an independent and self-enclosed self, we start to bother ourselves.

> Idea 2 – We fail to appreciate the
> mystery of life.

Allow me to speak for myself. I have been possessed by a kind of madness. This madness takes shape as a definite tendency to fixate on a person or way of life as my salvation. I abandon the ordinary; the day-to-day. I go for the highest, the most intense experiences, which allow me the most special and rarefied of self-images. I reject what is right in front of me, and situate passionate dedication into the receding future.

Oh alienating desire, that poison of the mind, which makes my my friends' faces foreign; the blue sky dull, food tasteless, and my passions mere shades, however fervently I pursue them! When I am in this particular, er, *frame of mind*, I keep trying to get to the part of the story where the heartache stops, as Gordon Lightfoot would say. And when I finally manage to stop this, or, to use my favorite phrase, when I finally "start stopping," *here* is the mystery. Right here.

These crows cawing outside my window, have they always been here? And what about this rain, making soft riplets in the puddles on the walk?

> Idea 3 - We *can* stop trying to get
> something *out* of life.

Striving for perfection, the compulsion to manufacture a perfect situation, is a habit with us. We are addicted to improving ourselves and our lives' situations. But we cannot experience our true openness by improving ourselves. It is a bit like taking better and better care of our bodies; eating nothing but brown rice and vegetables and running marathons and so on, and doing all this in the hope that one day we will be able to fly.

If this is our attitude, we will assume that flying is superior to walking, although flying is not natural to the human body. We might even decide we won't really feel alive until we can fly. If we live like this, we will fail to notice and enjoy our actual, superb health.

> 'If you say the Kingdom of God is in the
> sky, then the birds got in ahead of you.'
> – Jesus of Nazareth, *The Gospel of Thomas*.

The fact is, we can't improve and improve, and finally get to ourselves. It won't work and it's not necessary. We are already ourselves. A word of warning before we move on: there are some people who would capitalize on your compulsion for perfection.

These folks will help you experience your true nature as open awareness, then yank it away by telling you you've got to read the next book, attend the next workshop, or advance to the next level. Don't buy it. By situating freedom in some future event that they will control, these teachers are stealing your wallet and helping you look for it.

> Idea 4 – We *can* be awake and intimately in touch with the mystery of present-moment experience.

Appreciation of the mystery of life is not another state that we have to attain. It is merely the knowledge and acceptance that there is really nowhere else we have to go, nothing else we have to do. Now, there *are* feeling-states which I associate with this freedom and this appreciation of the mystery of life. They a kind-of pervasive, loving poignancy, and a gentle sense of curiosity or surprise. But these are not states of a person, as

I would define a person.

Isn't the idea of personhood based on a sense of will and control? Isn't the self in charge of something? Doesn't it have a sphere of influence? Isn't the self what it takes itself to be, in opposition to what it does not take itself to be? Doesn't the self push away its objects of desire by considering them to be objects, even as it seems to draw them near by desiring them?

By contrast, these poignant feelings come, not from a subject, but from an unbounded openness, which wants only what is happening now. This unbounded openness does not look for satisfaction in the next person, emotion, or thought. It seems to accept every situation as is.

Some have called this openness "renunciation." This is not the "I give up" of a discouraged self, however. This is the dissolution of the self-enclosed self – and the realization that there never was any self-enclosed self to begin with.

Idea 5 – We *can* understand philosophically that present-moment experience is the only 'thing' there is.

Q: What gives the "illumined ones" peace of mind?
A: Nothing does. The very search for any subjective state fuels discontent. The "illumined ones" experience peace and joy because they have been willing to abandon an innately disturbing illusion.

The 'illumined ones' experience a feeling of peaceful, open awareness because they have given something up in exchange for it. They have given up the occasional pleasure they receive from promoting a brittle and rather high-maintenance sense of self. They experience peace because they have been willing to discard an innately disturbing illusion: the illusion that there is a self which needs to be 'realized' or 'fulfilled.' This illusion results in our common compulsion to change our current situations.

Because we identify with our desires, we situate our freedom in our ability to pursue and fulfill desires. But then we are stuck with our desires. Consider the case of someone who has been imprisoned. At the end of her sentence, a guard opens the prison door and she is at liberty to pursue her desires. But she is not necessarily free with regard to her desires. She has *liberty* to pursue desires, but she may not have the *freedom* to choose whether she will pursue her desires or not.

If we want to appreciate the mystery of life, it is essential to evade the compulsion of our desires by understanding that there does not *need* to be anything else in our current situations. There is no greater feeling, state, or condition that we have to achieve. There is no lesser or more limited feeling, state, or condition that we have to be liberated from. This is it. And this poignancy is always here. We can give ourselves permission to experience it; to be right here with it. To be available to it. To be available to the mystery of life is to be free.

Get it? No? OK, let's investigate this important idea a little more closely. When we long for things, it happens that we become very good at longing. So why won't we keep right on longing after we get what we want? When our desired conditions are finally met, they can't take away our habit of longing, so they come too late. When we have to make an appointment with life, we are always late for our appointment.

Alienating desire can obscure our felt contact with the mystery of life. Take getting a new, 'perfect' partner. Aren't we giddy with joy? The reason we are giddy with joy is because joy is our genuine nature. We just abandoned it for a little while because we were busy bothering ourselves with fantasies. We can experience profound joy if we give ourselves permission to. Instead we look outside ourselves for a perfect situation. And it is the act of looking that takes us away from our happiness.

Think of the driven person. When she gets what she wants, she is already overreaching it to have it forever. When even having it forever won't do, she abandons the very person, position, or accomplishment she once so fervently sought, and she is no longer present even to them. She is not available.

We want to get away from our self-created feelings of dissatisfaction by following the track of these feelings and trying to get things to turn out the way we imagine they should. It *is* possible to experience the mystery of our dissatisfaction itself - to be intimate with it - and to refuse to abandon it. We are not very good at this. Instead we follow this feeling like a Pied Piper. We allow it to hoodwink us with the illusory promise that if we give it what it wants, it will go away.

Take the example of anger. Anger is an energizing reaction. As such, anger may have safeguarded the survival of our species, no small achievement! But anger doesn't do the one thing it seems to promise. Satisfying our angry impulses does not lead to the dissipation of these impulses. In fact, if we give vent to anger frequently, we may get fixated on anger. We may get addicted to angry outbursts, and to the experience of anger itself. Anger is a comparatively simple example. Our spiritual impulses are much more complex.

When we create the desire for inner improvement and psychological states of peace, we sometimes notice, (if we are lucky), that we are causing our own dissatisfaction. We usually then create a psychology to eliminate it. We try to have more

25

compassion and acceptance for ourselves and others. Well, what could possibly be wrong with this? Nothing, except that when problems persist, our standard solutions to these problems are often part of the problems themselves.

Acceptance, compassion, and the various antidotes to our self-bothering and dissatisfaction definitely diminish it. But this is a lengthy process requiring enormous dedication. Like the problem of simple substances in physics – each particle of dissatisfaction turns out to be another compound. Dissatisfaction can be broken down into ever smaller particles. And infinitesimal dissatisfaction turns out to be as vexing a problem as infinite dissatisfaction was. We find that we end up scrubbing our hands all day like Lady Macbeth, trying to shed smaller and smaller particles of anger, jealousy and regret.

The fact is, we don't experience the mystery of life by 'working through' our perturbation. We just experience it. We simply decide to experience life, without judgment or expectation. A moment's lapse is a moment's lapse. The reason our occasional, alienating thoughts and feelings bother us is because we think we should be bothered by them.

Chances are we have adopted a rather grandiose identity as someone who "has peace" all the time. Do you see the irony here? When we try to overcome reactive emotions, there is always the infinitesimal remainder we can never be rid of. We are then like a rocket attempting to break the speed of light, which can never burn enough fuel to push the weight of its fuel to light speed.

Wakefulness or enlightenment can be reasonably defined as appreciating the mystery of life in the present moment, while knowing it is the only 'thing' there is. Wakefulness' opposite – the dissatisfaction brought about by reactive emotions and alienating desire – can be reasonably defined as the futile attempt to 'get something out of life.'

We can not get anything out of life. There is no outside where we could take this thing to. There is no little pocket situated outside of life, which would steal life's provisions and squirrel them away. The life of this moment has no outside.

So far, so good. We have taken a look at our sense of distraction from our awake, open clarity. Now let's take a look at this open clarity itself. What is the relationship between our original awake, open clarity, and the feeling or experience of "waking up?"

The Dream

The other night, I dreamt a tick was burrowing himself into my thigh. I grabbed hold of him with my fingers. I was able to pull him out by his legs before he could burrow into my skin. I took a pair of tweezers out of my medicine cabinet and carefully and thoroughly removed all the stray tick parts. Then I cleaned the little wound site out with soap. When I woke up my thigh was perfectly fine, with no trace of tick insertion. Not because I'd pulled the tick out so carefully, but because he had never existed in the first place.

Notice how 'fixing' fixed things in this example, but waking up revealed the original absence of any problem. It would be easy to assume that these two things are related somehow; "fixing" and "waking up." I am not sure that they are.

Q: How does a magician pull a rabbit out of a hat?
A: He put the rabbit in the hat in the first place.

How do we pull the illusion that there is some abiding and intractable "problem" with our lives, out of our lives? I would not be the first to suggest we do this by realizing that our sense of problem hangs on our sense of being a self who "has" a problem.

Our sense of being a self-enclosed self is the fundamental illusion, the magic trick which allows the story of our lives to unfold. But we are not this little self-enclosed, self-involved nugget of self. Our true self, our true 'I,' is open awareness; an open, loving field of experience.

Do you know those sliding tile puzzles they give to kids in restaurants? Where they have to get the numbered tiles to line up in a sequence? Our true 'I' is like the empty space in the sliding tile puzzle which allows the tiles to move. As a square-shaped opening, this empty space is roughly the dimensions of the other tiles. It looks like a tile made of space. But space is not a thing. There is no such thing as a rectangle-shaped bit of space. There is simply a gap between tiles, which allows them some mobility.

Our true 'I' is an open, empty 'field' which allows experience to manifest freely. When we no longer believe there is a self that must transcend itself and its circumstances, we have achieved the only real freedom there is – freedom from our illusory sense of bondage and confinement to the adventures of a self.

Let's look at an ordinary example. Do you want to move out of your dilapidated apartment? I sure do! But let's imagine ourselves at 95. How we would give anything to see this dilapidated apartment once more; to tenderly and reverently walk through its strange, gray halls.

This is the tenderness with which we can appreciate life now. It is the radical opposite of 'fixing' an apparent self and its problems. In poignant moments, including these moments of nostalgia, we feel life's fleeting and mysterious nature. We feel that this self barely hangs together, and is already almost gone.

This tender quality is not an experience of self-love *per se*. It is an experience of love in a profound, felt realization that the self is made of nothing other than present-moment experience, and is a precarious, dissolving thing. It is a "mist that hangs in the morning," as the Psalmist says. When we realize our true self is nothing other than present-moment experience, we are free to love whatever is happening, regardless of whether we like it!

If our partner rejects us, of course we will grieve his or her absence and do nothing for weeks but watch *Buffy the Vampire Slayer* in our ratty bathrobe. But we can grieve with the profound understanding that this moment of grieving is life here and now. This is it. This moment is what's happening now. Must we give in to the hoodwinking desire that tells us to abandon this moment because it is not what we wanted?

The Rainbow

We have discussed the kinds of distractions which seem to take us away from present experience. We have discussed how waking up, or getting clear, involves the dissolution of false assumptions which support our dissatisfaction, and does not involve fixing an apparent self and her problems.

So, what are these false assumptions? And what is the actual mechanism of our dissatisfaction? How does it get the job done? How does it get us to experience the mystery of life only in the briefest of flashes, like fingers of light breaking through the clouds in a Flemish painting, illuminating a mere inch of the landscape here and there?

The mechanism of dissatisfaction is not a real entity. It is an apparition like a rainbow. A rainbow is a beam of light which has been refracted through water droplets in the air and reflected in the retina of the eye. The illusion of the rainbow is that it ends just a few yards away, where we can go and stand in its multicolored light.

The "real" rainbow exists literally in the eye of the beholder. The band of the rainbow does not stretch across an actual horizon, but is found literally in our own eye.

We can photograph rainbows because light reflects in a camera lens in a similar manner. Like the shadows in Plato's cave, the rainbow is on the inside. Yet we chase it.

There is a pervasive feeling of poignancy. It is like the cosmic hum; the radiation left over after the Big Bang. It is always present. It is the feeling of existence. We recognize ourselves as open awareness when we stand in the mystery of this feeling. This is our true nature, our open heart. We are searching for this total openness. We're running from it, too.

We are seeking the very thing we're running from; running from the very thing we're seeking. Anger, jealousy, regret, anxiety and obsessive desire, the so-called "reactive" emotions, attempt to defend us against this primary poignancy. Our usual *modus operandi* is to project this poignancy onto another person or situation. We imagine we have a solid identity with clear likes and dislikes. We become a person who has clearly defined situations and people she wants and pursues, and situations and people she dislikes and despises.

We then experience a predictable sense of excitement when we get close to something we want, and a predictable feeling of disdain when we feel a situation we want nothing to do with coming on. Caught in fantasies which support our preferred identities, we also shut off a good portion of our actual experience. A good portion of our lives, (let's say 90%, just to be dramatic), don't register at all. And then we feel cut-off from life as if we are living behind a pane of glass.

This very attitude causes the dissatisfaction we feel. And unfortunately, we seek happiness in the very heart of our dissatisfaction. We look for happiness in the heart of longing, and we just get more interesting longing. When we get the job we want, we find ourselves wanting to want something else again. To be able to feel this poignancy and not turn away from it; this would be the felt aspect of Wakefulness. To know true intimacy and not try to hide in the illusory redoubt of the self would be Wakefulness. To not go and find the little reeds and straws of additional excitement and status to build the nest of the self-enclosed self would be Wakefulness.

Wakefulness is the Alpha and the Omega. It is what we are running from. It is also what we are seeking. We are escaping from the very thing we're trying to get to.

We are aspiring to the very thing we're trying to escape!

We try to run from the poignancy at the heart of existence into plans, projects, fantasies, worries, regrets, and images of serenity and peace. Or we try to perfect it, 'tweak' it somehow. But it is already perfect, in that it transcends any concept we would have of it. If we must have a project, we can appreciate the mystery of existence without trying to resolve it into a specific feeling or understanding we will then articulate, control and repeat.

For example, we try to abandon our lives by aspiring to experience their mystery fully in the future, or in some distant and exotic locale. We lead treks to the Himalayas because we are certain we can find a little extra mystery there. It doesn't matter what we do, so long as we keep the rainbow's end just out of reach.

When I was 23 I had one of those life-defining infatuations. Somehow I knew if I received an impassioned letter from the object of my crush, I would wait a good three days before responding. And those three days would be some of the most exciting of my life. (Notice the word "excitement" has *ex* as its prefix, 'to be outside of a state or condition.')

In a certain sense, there really is nothing more exciting than entertaining a fantasy.

Fantasy is exciting. It is also insular. It consists of the impossible project of trying to take a break from the intimacy of reality. The major purpose of our fantasies is usually to delay or even prevent real intimacy! This is why I sometimes refer to this kind of fantasy as 'alienating desire.' Alienating desire is any desire which drains reality from life. In fact, is it really desire? Do we really want our desires to "come true?" Or is it just desire for desire; the desire to remain in desire, and separate from the object of our desire?

If I were to hold on to a fantasy indefinitely, it would become more and more empty, repetitive, and stagnant. But despite its obvious shortcomings, I could hold on to it. These reflections bring us to an understanding of what poignancy is, and why experience is suffused with this sublime yet bittersweet feeling. Living experience is poignant because it is composed of 'can't hold on.'

As the Buddha stated in his sutra on the three marks of existence, living experience is precarious, deeply unsatisfying when viewed from the perspective of our projects and desires, and without essence, offering nothing to hold on to. We may think we are bound by our lives' experiences. But as soon as we touch them, they dissolve. We think we have to search for freedom. Really there is nothing else.

The Sun

'I do not see the sun, but I see an eye that sees the sun.' – Arthur Schopenhauer

We experience dissatisfaction when we live our lives to further our ambitions, entertain fantasies, or at least avoid unpleasantness. Why can't we live our lives to reach the noble goal of self-transcendence? This is an important question, and I think it will help to investigate it thoroughly. Our investigation will concern our belief in a radically self-enclosed self: the belief that causes our troubles.

Is there a self? What is its nature? Why does it need to transcend itself? In what direction, exactly, should it transcend itself? It is hard to point to the self because it seems to be everywhere we look. As Schopenhauer put it so eloquently in the above quotation, everywhere I look I see my own seeing, my own perception. I don't even see my own partner, but I see my own perception of my partner. We might as well say that 'others exist only insofar as I perceive them.' But we would be a little duped by the structure of language here.

It is true that I cannot reach another person with any means but my own perception. If I were to reach a person named Ichabod Jones, I would have to see him, touch him, hear him, or, but hopefully not, smell him. I could also talk with other people about him. But this also involves my own hearing and seeing. I simply cannot get in touch with him in any location that would exist beyond or outside of my experience.

Experience is the only place where the self and others appear. "Experience" is another word for the way in which things appear. They appear in certain ways that are regulated by our senses of sight, hearing, smell, etc. Because we experience nothing outside of our own experience, experience is a pretty totalizing concept, isn't it? Do we really need to call it anything? It's like when you ask someone, "How's life?" and they say, "Compared to what?" It's like a fish trying to describe water, isn't it?

A couple hundred years ago, Western philosophers became interested in the fact that we know the world only by means of our own experience. Some said we experience by means of certain inviolable categories of experience, by space and time for example. This is notably the view of Immanuel Kant. Our experience of space and time, he argued, does not arise from the side of the world.

It arises from the way our minds constitute experience. These categories are constitutive of the possibility of experience itself. We experience the world *by means of* space and time.

These ideas were profoundly influential, and have been called the Copernican Turn in philosophy. Indicating that this shift in philosophy was just as radical as the literal turn to a heliocentric solar system in physics. Just as the sun does not revolve around the earth, but the other way 'round, so our perception is not governed by the objects we perceive. Rather, objects are perceived according to our perception.

Do we perceive just *according* to our perception, or do we *just* perceive our own perception? What does reality look like when we're not looking? Some claim there is an unknowable reality outside of our experience of reality. Others assert, (notably the phenomenologist Edmund Husserl), that our perception of things, and things as they would be anyway, apart from our perception, are one and the same. Since we cannot, in any case, get out of our experience, what is the usefulness, they ask, of positing a distinction between what we perceive, and things as they would be apart from our perception?

These observations lead to an additional question: if what I perceive is *just* my own perception, does it follow that I perceive *myself* when I look at things? I don't think it does follow. In fact, the question I just asked describes a philosophical position that is sometimes called "mentalism." "Mentalism" is the logical opposite of materialism, and maintains many of materialism's unquestioned assumptions.

In the materialistic view, our perception mirrors an external world of solid objects out there. In the mentalistic view, the external world is thought to be a gossamer projection of the perceiver's mind. In the materialistic view, the world pre-exists, at least theoretically, our perception of it. In the mentalistic view, a mind pre-exists, at least theoretically, our perception of a world. In the first view, we look out at the world to learn about the world. In the second, we look out at an apparent external world to learn about ourselves.

When we understand that an individual experiences only according to the capacities of her experiencing mind, we *could* assume that this individual's world of experience is her mind. And then we could ask interesting questions about whether this individual can control her world as she controls her mind.

We can't really control our minds though, can we? Can we control our moods? What about our thoughts? Our actions? When a hand reaches out to that earthenware coffee mug with the cobalt ring, is that a clear act of will? Or does it, in some sense, just happen? And if a thought arises, "I should really lay off the coffee," and the hand stops in mid-course, are we absolutely certain that this thought *caused* the interruption of the hand's habitual course?

In addition to believing that they should eventually be able to control all events that take place in their worlds, those who take a mentalistic view may also be tempted to believe such statements as, "I must be a really evil person, if such evil things are happening in the world!" I do not believe that this concern is necessary. Mentalism's insight that the world is not different from the mind is a radical and interesting one. Good and evil are properties of independent selves, however. I do not find it necessary to posit such selves, who would then be implicated in the moral drift of their projected universes.

To avoid such extreme and disturbing positions, 1 think it is best to dissolve the concepts of 'world' and 'mind' and have done with them. We can question these concepts at a very basic level. If I take seriously the idea that I experience the world only according to my own perceptual capacities, then who is to say that this perception is located in my 'eyes,' which are themselves only perceived insofar as I perceive them, for example by looking in the mirror?

'Consciousness,' 'perception' (these terms are themselves rather weird reifications, or weird *nounings,* of the experience 'to be conscious of,' 'to perceive') do not necessarily exist in the head, do they? Perception is the very fabric of experience! How could it exist in a head? [1]

Conscious experience is total. We can't get out of it. But just when we start feeling oppressed by experience's totality, and start positing an outside, (and such positing is usually based on a misunderstanding of language and language's tendency to divide things into opposites), we notice that experience does not hang together very well. Experience is not a thing the way rocks are things.

I just described experience as an all-containing fabric. But that's only a metaphor. Experience is nothing other than

---

[1] Many people have made this point eloquently, most notably Ludwig Wittgenstein in his later works, and Douglas Harding.

here and now, what's happening. What's happening? The happening of 'what's happening' has no extension. It does not point outside of itself.

Our memories of past events are actually occurring as present experience. Our perfectly rational anticipations of future events are also taking place as present experience. Just when we start to feel oppressed by the fact that presently arising experience is the only 'thing' there is, what was once here is already gone. And what is here now is completely unrelated to anything that went on here before. Or maybe it is related. But we can't prove it.

If you saw two people playing catch in a dream, could you really say that one person caught the ball *because* the other one threw it? In waking life we say these things all the time. And they are true as far as they go. But they are assumptions. All we really perceive is present experience. And we cannot prove the existence of any container which makes experience hang together.

As we discussed before, just because thoughts arise, it does not follow that they take place in a "mind," and certainly not in a head. Just because events arise, it does not follow that they take place in a "world." I think we can dispense with these conventional containers when they become unwieldy. Instead, can we just take a look at what is given?

If we just notice the *fact* that we only perceive by means of our own perception – that in this sense and this sense only we never escape our own experience – intriguing questions arise. Sooner or later, someone will question the dividing line between the self and her experience, and other people and her experience of them.

When we develop theories and concepts about the nature of reality, these concepts usually presuppose the existence of these dividing lines, even where they re-draw them. Can we soften these lines? Can we soften the difference between the self and her experience? Can we notice that we do not actually see these lines anywhere in our looking? Interesting things happen when we just look at experience, without attaching boundaries and concepts.

We could say that experience is "beyond concepts," but even that is to define it. To draw another line. It's not in France, so it must be in Belgium. Experience cannot be described. Not from a vantage point outside of it! Just because experience cannot be described, that doesn't mean we can trap it in our cricket box called "indescribable" and make it sing for us all night. We all experience plenty of things that are indescribable, but that doesn't put them on a par with experience itself any more than my mother calling me "impossible" makes me a square circle.

We could call experience "beyond description," as long as we understand that this phrase is not being used to refer to an abstract, temporarily unexplored territory of description. "Experience" is that which cannot be described or defined because there is simply no place outside of it from which we could do the describing.

We often pretend there is such a place, don't we? We think that the 'self' is such a vantage. We think we can describe experience from the vantage of a 'self.' Or we pretend that this vantage is somehow situated in another person. We pretend that a hole opens up in experience whenever somebody walks by, through which we can glimpse another dimension, as if through the pinpoint aperture in a shoebox diorama.

There are a couple of ways we can put the match to these illusions. We can explore how the creation of a self, or 'selving' is actually accomplished, through introspection and through self-description; that is, by observing how we actually describe ourselves.

This approach has its dangers, however. When we use it, we tend to say, "See? There is such a thing as a self! I can describe it in great detail!"

Fortunately, we can also note that the feeling of self is not always present. We can notice – deeply observe – instances when the feeling of self is absent, and there is just consciousness, experience, or 'this.' In a moment, we will take a look at some of these instances. For now, let's just notice that we artificially, if at times usefully, divide experience into self and not-self. It isn't always clear where we should put that line, is it? Is my body my self? What about the air I breathe?

Often we get very interested in studying ourselves, without pausing to notice that we have arbitrarily defined one part of experience as our self, and not another. To give a simple example, a sunny day usually puts us in a good mood, at least in New England. And I've heard Scandinavians practically go manic! Is there any reason to separate our good mood from the sunlight itself? Is there any absolute reason to say that our good mood is somehow the property of a self, and the sunlight is somehow other? Can we not imagine a language in which 'sunlight' refers to being in a good mood, and not metaphorically?

I believe there is no great reason to maintain the concept of self beyond its obvious usefulness as a designator. The 'self' as a metaphysical concept, or a concept that would set itself up to be a great, absolute truth, is much too high-maintenance. It simply cannot be made to exist beyond our everyday attempts at self-definition and self-description.

Let's review where we have been before we take a look at experiences where the illusion of boundary lines between the experiencer, her experience and the objects of her experience is entirely absent.

We have given up the idea that experience is different from reality as it would be anyway, apart from our experience of it. Though some would say perception is like seeing in a mirror, dimly – even they have to admit it is not a mirror we can ever get outside of. So let's allow that to be as it is. Our experience of reality is all the reality we are going to get. There is no real life which is elsewhere.

We have also discovered that experience does not belong to an individual who experiences. That would be again to posit an outside, something apart from experience. An outlet. An inner outlet (a self, mind, head, brain, unconscious, soul) which exists over and against an outer outlet (someone else's mind, the world, the future, the past, 'reality,' the outside).

'Selving' is at best not terribly necessary. And at worst we create a monster, as selving can become a futile attempt to abandon experience! We begin to prefer positing a self and her conditions, and "fixing" the one or the other, over actual experience, which does not consist of selves and their conditions, and which is the only 'thing' there is.

When we are 'selving,' we are abandoning what we actually see, hear, and feel (which is always dissolving, always falling apart) in favor of concepts, which hold together nicely, but which are mere conventions. When we just look at experience; when we observe it closely, we do not discover any selves. In fact, when we observe experience carefully and non-selectively, it does slowly dawn on us that no one is home.

The Comet

Let's take a look at some actual experiences. They are experiences which I have selected, somewhat at random, because the usual, presumed line between me as subject, my experiences, and their supposed objects is nowhere to be found. Of course, as we have already discussed, it never *is* anywhere to be found. But we don't usually pause long enough to notice this.

Sometimes the only way to articulate these experiences is to put them in language that sounds sacred or mystical. So we might categorize them as sacred experiences. They are certainly instructive experiences! But they are not, for this reason, anything special.

Remember how Foghorn Leghorn says, "Listen to me when I'm talking to you, boy!" In that spirit, let me remind you that *all experiences are experiences of awakening*. Every experience points to the truth if you look at it closely enough.

Radically Condensed Instructions

When I was little, 6 or 7, I used to turn our wicker laundry hamper upside-down, and stand on it so I could look at myself in the bathroom mirror. I would stare at the little face in the mirror until I experienced a feeling of alienation. I knew the little face staring at me from the mirror was not me. But it was not not-me. I knew I was not localized in this face, or limited by this face. That's why staring at myself felt so creepy. I knew that I was, and was not, this face. And I just could not reduce myself to one alternative or the other.

I was a teenager, maybe 11 or 12. I was lying on my back looking up into the branches of my grandmother's weeping willow. Yellow-green leaves sparkled against the topaz sky. I found myself thinking: "in order to really see how perfect this is, I must have been here forever!" This thought seemed to express a sense of familiarity, of intimacy, in my perception of the beauty of the tree. It was as if the tree's beauty and my perception of it were not entirely separate creatures, but were intimately intertwined and were in some way recognizing each other.

The Comet

When I was 19, I had a conversation with my philosophy professor about human nature. This happened in the already-dark of an early evening in winter. My professor introduced the idea that people are basically good and we are all doing the best we can. This is a fairly common notion in progressive philosophical circles, but not one I had heard before. Until then, I'd assumed the world is divided between good and not-so-good types. I hadn't considered that, though limited in some ways, we all share the same basic good intentions. It had simply never occurred to me that others' insides are similar to, perhaps the same, as mine. That others' feeling of themselves might be exactly the same as mine. Might *be* mine.

I walked out of his office, feeling an expansive and warm feeling in the center of my chest. I looked back at the building I had just left, appreciating our conversation. When I did, I saw shining white and indigo lights over this academic building, Aspinwall, in appearance like a comet whose tail spiraled across the horizon. Given the sense of lightness and joy I felt from my previous insights, I surmised it was my own mind, my own consciousness I was seeing. It had that "feel."

Besides, nobody else was stopping to look at the comet!

At the time I wasn't the least bit worried that I was having a minor hallucination. What 19-year-old worries about anything? But I did recognize the enormous implications of seeing my own consciousness spread across the evening sky. "If the comet is just my own consciousness," I wondered, "what about Aspinwall? Why isn't it the case that Aspinwall is just my own consciousness, too? This would be pretty unlikely. But it's not impossible, is it? Does anything absolutely prevent it? What about my friends? What about, *ack*, my own body, my own self?"

For a few days after this experience, I searched desperately for something that I knew to exist distinctly and absolutely outside of my conscious experience. All day long I had conversations with myself that went like this:

"Those actors on TV, they're not my consciousness, are they?
Well, who is seeing them? Where do they exist, but in my consciousness?
How about Pluto? Does it exist out there in space?
Of course it does. Where else would it be?

But does it truly exist outside of my experience of it? Outside of my hearing about it in elementary school, for example? If I actually went and saw it, what would that *prove*?"

And to give my favorite example: one crystalline fall day not long ago, I looked intently at my writing desk. Now, I don't want you to think I'm a lunatic, but I would be remiss not to tell you that my writing desk was saying "hi" to me. It was greeting me. It was not jumping up and down; writing desks do not generally jump up and down. But it was clearly saying its own kind of "hello." Nowadays I would probably use the term self-luminosity. My writing desk was shining in its own self-luminosity. But "saying hi" works just as well.

When we start to lose our hard-and-fast sense of self, we may feel that we are losing touch with objective reality. But we need not worry. There is no such thing as objective reality! There is only experience. And the whole point of experience is to be intimate with us. It *is* us. Saying 'hi' to us is all it does. Experience is nothing other than a continual acknowledgment. My writing desk's very existence is a kind of greeting. Hello!

I am not saying for an instant that the world is a kind of strange, private dream. I am not saying that reality is a dream, and certainly not a private one. I am saying that whatever you think the world's status is, the fact is, that the 'self' who would be dreaming, (or really seeing things as they are), is an artificial program we are running, which takes up an inordinate amount of energy. In fact it's a real pain in the neck.

When we question our belief that we "have" a self, the concept of private experience is challenged as well. Consider the case of artificial awakening. Artificial awakening occurs when we feel like we just woke up, and we go about our ordinary activities like making coffee and brushing our teeth.

We notice there is something wrong with our surroundings. Details are wrong. Should this painting be on that wall? A sense of uncanniness pervades our experience. A sense of "wrongness" is soaked into the very walls and furniture. Then we wake up in our bed, and realize we dreamt the whole thing.

Or consider the movie *The Matrix*. In *The Matrix*, human beings are not living out our lives as free individuals. Instead we are confined to pods, being fed sensory experiences that some mischievous computers have programmed to make us think we are free, so they won't have a rebellion on their hands. In this movie, the character Neo senses there is something wrong with his reality, by experiencing the same sense of pervasive uncanniness that people who experience artificial awakening report.

In both of these examples, there seems to be a hidden component to experience; something experience isn't telling us. This hidden component would of course be that the experience is not "real," and the things we do inside it do not ultimately matter. These interpretations assume, however, that there are human brains somewhere, asleep in the first case, and in electrical pods in the second, which produce *subjectivity*. The unexamined assumption here is that *we* are real; our subjectivity is real. We really exist, just somewhere else. We do not co-occur or co-arise with experience.

We get very preoccupied with levels of reality, and try desperately to discover what is "really real." And yet even in our deepest philosophical musings, we often forget to question the very idea of a self who experiences reality. Our standard theory of dreaming, (or of being imprisoned in a matrix where computers live on our electrical energy and body heat), is that we think we are experiencing an external reality, when "really" our reality is entirely internal, entirely private. No other real person could verify that we actually experience what we think we experience. This is because no other real person is in there with us.

If we found any clues pointing to the hidden duplicity of our experience, we would do everything possible to sniff it out. While deeply questioning the reality of our experience, however, we leave the strange concept that there is a self who exists elsewhere, in a condition utterly divorced from her experience, completely unquestioned.

The Mystery

We think there is something our experience isn't telling us. But experience is called 'the given' because everything is given. We think we are going to follow our experience, like a trail of breadcrumbs, to a self or another who is at least partially hidden, by the past or the future, or by our ignorance of reality. But nothing is hidden.

What do we believe is hidden? We think the past, or aspects of it, are hidden. But the past is nothing other than present memory. We think the future is hidden. But the future is nothing other than present anticipation, however realistic it seems. We think the unconscious content of our minds, "the unconscious," is hidden. But when we come into contact with what we think is "unconscious," through dreams, for example, we are conscious of it.

We think other people's minds are hidden. We think the truth is hidden. We think enlightenment is hidden. We think this of anything presumed far away and needing to be sought. Of anything presumed lost and needing to be found. Of anything presumed veiled and needing to be revealed

We think the self is hidden. This is why we have so many questions about what it is. We think of it as a kind of fortress or redoubt. And from this primary, presumed redoubt, comes our belief in all other essentially hidden and esoteric things.

The 'self' is a concept which operates almost continually in our lives. The 'self' concept boils down to the belief that there is a subject who exists somewhat apart from, somewhat distanced from, her experience. Therefore there is something missing from experience; there is a hidden component to experience.

There is *no* hidden component to experience. There is no mystery anywhere to be uncovered. It is all the mystery. And it is right here, already uncovered. Its existence co-arises with, and is the same as, its manifestation. Its 'hereness.'

From our unquestioned belief in a hidden self, flows our belief that there is a hidden meaning to this self's existence. Or a self-transcending state of enlightenment that this self should reach. This idea is false, and highly disturbing. It drains the life out of life.

We *can* understand, however, that there is no self-enclosed self who exists in separation from her experience of life. This understanding has been compared, rather smartly I think, with waking up.

When we wake up from a dream, we understand that all aspects of the dream were nothing other than our own experience. The dream self and the dream were one and the same. It was all experience. We may study it as closely as we like. We may look at it literally with a microscope. If you were to look at an apple slice under a microscope in a dream, you would see apple cells (unless it were a very whimsical dream!) But when you wake up you will not look for these apple slices under your pillow. You will know they were nothing other than your experience.

We could have the biggest problem going, and I mean the biggest neurotic obsession imaginable, and still it is all nothing but present experience. This understanding is completely liberating, once we get used to it.

There are no solid and abiding subjects and objects of experience, which are divided from each other as if by a pane of glass. Experience is nothing other than unbounded, undivided, awake and aware Consciousness.

Let's go back to our previous question: "What is the relationship between feeling awake to the mystery of present-moment experience and feeling dissatisfied and numb?" Feeling numb to experience is caused by the false perception that you are caught in the wrong experience, as if in a predicament. This perception is caused in turn by the false belief that you are a self who *pursues* experience. You do not need to *pursue* experience. You *are* experience.

The idea that we are selves who pursue is a very ill-advised kind of fantasy. The notion that we are selves pursuing experience sucks the sense of wonder out of life. The whole idea of being a 'self' is already a kind-of philosophical self-protection. It is the false idea of an abiding redoubt or enclosure in experience, which will remain fundamentally untouched and unaffected.

We adopt this notion of self because we think it will make us invulnerable. Instead it puts us profoundly at risk. Our image of this self-enclosed self is not just a blank. We project all of our preferred identities onto it. When these preferred identities do not manifest in this present instant, we believe we must chase them down, as if our very lives depend on this chase. But they don't. Only our fragile and ultimately illusory identities depend on our strange and heated pursuits.

The fact is, we do not need to be frantically absorbed in fantasies of experiences which will supposedly happen a little later on and over there. Everything we are and everything we need is here. And it happens all the time.

Summary and Conclusion

Open, perfect clarity subtends all experience. It *is* experience. Experience happens as an experiencing Awareness. Since experience does not happen anywhere else besides this Awareness, we know there is nothing else going on besides Awareness. Awareness is aware of itself!

I sometimes call experience 'Awareness' with a capital 'A,' so you know I mean business. We could also call it Consciousness, Being, Presence or Self. I mildly prefer 'Awareness' because it does not connote an object or process. But we don't really have to call it anything. We just need some term, some designator, to draw attention to what is always present. We know we do not and can not exist apart from Awareness. We know that even in our worst and most neurotic moments, we never leave the openness of the here-and-now, which is the only 'thing' there is. And yet we also understand it is best for us to simply 'be here, now.'

How do we live with this apparent paradox, this apparent conundrum? I believe that a profound understanding of Awareness is therapeutic in and of itself. It's true: even in our most obsessive, neurotic fantasies and fixations, we never leave present-moment experience, the only 'thing' there is. However, when we understand and accept that this present, awake experience is the only 'thing' that truly exists, we lose motivation to pursue our grandiose identities and disturbing obsessions.

It doesn't always happen all at once. Our obsessions might go on for a little while, like a bicycle whose rider has jumped off. But they simply cannot be sustained when the false sense of self which sustains them has been thoroughly repudiated and put out to hay.

Our real experience is one of open awareness. We feel bothered in distinction to our true reality, because we actively bother ourselves. The fact that we feel bothered from time to time doesn't mean anything, at least not metaphysically. Experience is infinite: we can have any experience we want as long as we are willing to put up with the consequences. Awareness is certainly not bothered because a self has been posited which chooses to bother itself.

We are absolutely, totally, and perfectly one with our nature as Awareness the instant we desist from bothering ourselves. That's enlightenment. There is really nothing we must do or become. We are enlightened anyway, but not always in a way we touch into.

Summary and Conclusion

Meditating, relaxing and spending time with a teacher can stop us temporarily from bothering ourselves, but our customary thinking will bring it right back. At these times, we feel we have "lost" contact with ourselves as open awareness or present experience. For this reason, it is helpful to understand theoretically how the present moment, our present encounter with life, is the only life there is. Distraction and self-bothering tempt us with untrue pictures of reality. In these untrue pictures, the subject-object duality is brought back and upheld in a subtle and unquestioned way.

Learning to stop ourselves from bothering ourselves is no different from learning to stop any other negative habit. A person who suffers from alcoholism, for example, may be able to stop drinking for a few hours. To persist in sobriety, however, she will need an adequate understanding of her disorder. She will need an effective philosophy.

An effective relapse prevention philosophy reduces the rate of relapse by reducing the overwhelming time-dimension of addiction. Instead of worrying about staying sober for the rest of their lives, alcohol-dependent people are wisely encouraged to stop drinking for one day, or one hour. They are told not to worry about the next hour or day.

This philosophy directly counteracts the hoodwinking nature of the desire for alcohol, which tells the sufferer she should drink now, because she is not able to stop drinking for a month, year, or lifetime now, and the drink will help her prepare for sobriety in the future. Her new perspective encourages her to be sober just for today. She may drink as much as she likes tomorrow. But tomorrow never comes.

Our global change in perspective works in a similar manner. Instead of concerning ourselves with the fact that we feel dissatisfied, not peaceful, and not particularly self-realized, our new perspective encourages us to return to the mystery of the present moment now.

Supported by our new perspective, we remember that our hope of future enlightenment is just another distortion in the fun-house mirror of our incorrect belief in the self and its future endeavors. We recall that the present moment is all there is, and that reality happens here alone. There is no external basis, therefore, from which we can evaluate our present experience.

Summary and Conclusion

When we feel reassured that our present emotional state does not matter quite like we thought it did, (because we have stopped using it to uphold a brittle self-image or identity), we are able to relax, and we are more in touch with the present moment. We no longer worry ourselves terribly about what we need to do to get to a state of self-realization. And from the perspective of Awareness, of course nothing really changed!

We believe that we need to wake up. But this belief is just a changing experience within experience itself. It is in structure no different from the belief that we need to trek to the Himalayas, or fit into a size 6, preferably before trekking to the Himalayas! This belief can be an effective stepping stone, if it gets us to question our false and often torturous assumptions, possibly even in the Himalayas.

But in its darker, less innocent aspects, the belief that we need to wake up can be something of a wolf in sheep's clothing. When we entertain it, we keep trying to pinch ourselves and wake up *from* present-moment experience, rather than appreciating the mystery of present-moment experience. The present moment is perfect in that it is a perfect mystery. Experience is beautifully, sacredly and non-conceptually perfect, in this present moment, now.

J Jennifer Matthews studied philosophy, theology and ethics at the University of Louvain, Belgium and the Episcopal Divinity School of Cambridge, MA.

She works as a counselor and meditation instructor at the CASPAR Emergency Center in Cambridge, MA.

Printed in Great Britain
by Amazon